# Shaggy, Waggy Dogs

## (And Others)

by Stephanie Calmenson
Photographs by Justin Sutcliffe

Clarion Books/New York

We are grateful to all the wonderful people and dogs who gave their time to make this book possible. Special thanks to Jane Holtham, Sue Brisk, Sherry Halweil, Ted Thirlby, Olivia Thirlby, and Dougie. Thanks, too, to the A.S.P.C.A., New York City.

Clarion Books · a Houghton Mifflin Company imprint · 215 Park Avenue South, New York, NY 10003
Text copyright © 1998 by Stephanie Calmenson · Illustrations copyright © 1998 by Justin Sutcliffe
Note: The name Frisbee™ is an officially registered trademark.
The text is set in 20/28-point Minion condensed.

www.houghtonmifflinbooks.com

Printed in Singapore.

LIBRARY OF CONGRESS CATALOGING-IN-PUBLICATION DATA

Calmenson, Stephanie.
Shaggy, waggy dogs (and others) / by Stephanie Calmenson ; photographs by Justin Sutcliffe.
p.   cm.        Includes index.
Summary: Brief rhymes describe more than two dozen dog breeds. Includes an author's note with advice on choosing a dog as a pet.
ISBN 0-395-77605-8        PA ISBN 0-618-19466-5
1. Dog breeds—Juvenile literature. 2. Dogs—Juvenile literature. [1. Dog breeds. 2. Dogs. 3. Pets.]
I. Sutcliffe, Justin, ill. II. Title
SF426.5.C35    1998        97-33094
636.7'1—dc21        CIP
AC

TWP  10  9  8  7  6  5

To Rachel, Anna, and Pearl
—*S.C.*

To Jamie
—*J.S.*

I'm going on a dog walk.
I wonder what breeds I'll see.
I'm finally getting a dog of my own.
Which kind will be right for me?

# Poodle

Who just went to the groomer?
Who's looking very well?
Is it the mistress or the dog?
Neither one will tell.

## Afghan Hound

That dog isn't walking, he's bouncing!

He's bouncing down the street!

I wonder what's beneath the hair.

Are there springs inside his feet?

# Basset Hound

This dog is howling
A tune that I know.
The name of it is
"Do Your Ears Hang Low?"

# Bulldog

This dog is ugly-beautiful.

I see her and I smile.

Great big shoulders. Pushed-in face.

Oh, she has such style!

# Pembroke Welsh Corgi

Most of this dog
Is the usual sort
Till you get to his legs:
They're very short.

## Beagle

She's a very merry hunting dog,
Loved wherever she goes.
Just watch her or she'll wander off
While following her nose.

# Boxer

The name says these are fighters.

Their muscles say so too.

But what they really want

Is a chance to play with you.

# German Shepherd

He's smart, strong, handsome.

He likes working hard.

He can guide, herd, track,

Or be your loyal guard.

# Shar-Pei

Purple tongue,
Warm, brown eyes.
But his wrinkly coat
Looks too big for his size.

## Labrador Retriever

He cannot stop for petting.

He cannot stop to play.

This dog has a job to do.

He helps his mistress find her way.

# Bichon Frise

He's white like puffs of cotton.
His face is a happy surprise:
Out from his marshmallow hair
Peek two black-cherry eyes.

# Jack Russell Terrier

Catch that Frisbee. Wag that tail.

You're a dog who likes to play.

Tug that Frisbee. Don't let go.

You're a dog who'll play all day.

# Chinese Crested

She has some hair
On her head, paws, and tail.
The rest of this dog
Is as smooth as a snail.

# Tibetan Terrier

How can she see
Through all that hair?
Hello! Hello!
Is a dog in there?

# Newfoundland

Look who's just been swimming—
A happy, dripping pet.
Get out of the way when he shakes off,
Or you'll be very wet!

## Golden Retriever

If you throw the ball in the water,
He'll fetch it for you, and then—
If you throw the ball in the water,
He'll play the game again.

# Komondor

Do you see what I see?

A big walking mop.

His ropes of hair

Drop down from the top.

# Cocker Spaniel

He's a friendly dog
And handsome, too.
But ears in the water bowl
Just will not do!

# Rottweiler

This dog looks big,
Muscular, lean.
Please tell me fast—
Is he friendly or mean?

## Smooth Fox Terrier

She likes to dig, dig, dig

Down, down in the ground,

Then come up, up, up

With whatever she's found.

# Great Dane

I'm not sure I could walk him.
I just might be too small.
In case you hadn't noticed,
This dog is very TALL.

# Yorkshire Terrier

This dog is so small
She'd fit in a locket.
Well, maybe not quite—
Let's try a pocket.

## Soft-Coated Wheaten Terrier

One dog looks like the other.

This dog looks like that.

Same breed, different hairdos:

One is fluffy, one is flat.

# Norwich Terrier and Norfolk Terrier

Which dog is which?

They seem just the same.

Till you look at the ears,

Then the answer is plain.

*Norwich Terrier*                    *Norfolk Terrier*

# Vizsla

This dog is fast!
She was born to run.
See her gleaming coat—
Like a penny in the sun.

## Dalmatian

This dog is white
Where the spots are not.
But lots and lots
Of spots he's got.

# Australian Shepherd

His family herded cattle.

That's the reason why

He nips at heels and tries to herd

The people passing by.

## Schipperke

Ahoy, little captain.

Keep an eye on the ship.

You're a fine companion

For any sailing trip.

# Old English Sheepdog

Here's a happy dog
Who's big and shaggy.
Since he has no tail,
All of him gets waggy.

# Dachshund

Everyone says it,
So I'll say it too.
She looks like a hot dog—
Isn't it true?

Look! The animal shelter!
Which dog should I get?
One that's shaggy? Waggy? Spotted?
A hairless pet?

A herding dog?
One who catches a ball?
A dog who digs?
I want them all.

I got my dog! I love her!
What kind of dog is she?
A little of this and a little of that—
She's just the right dog for me.

## A Word About Breeds

In this book there are more than two dozen dog breeds. Two dozen may seem like a lot of choices, until you think about the more than four hundred breeds known today. What exactly is a breed? A breed is a group of dogs with offspring that look and behave like their parents. Like dogs themselves, the system of classifying dogs can be unruly. Breeds are often grouped together according to their function: herding, hunting, or companion dogs, for example. They are further grouped according to their appearance. The same breed may have several different names. Over time, as breeds are mixed, established breeds disappear and new breeds are formed.

# Which Dog Is Right for You?

Whatever breed—or mix of breeds—you choose, it is important to have the right dog for you. What does it mean to have the *right* dog? The right dog is the dog you can live with happily and care for well.

If you are someone who likes peace and quiet, you will probably have a hard time living happily with a yappy dog. If you live in a small city apartment and don't have time for long walks, you are not going to be the best caretaker for a dog who needs a lot of exercise.

Here are some of the things you will want to consider when choosing a dog:

- Size and appearance
- Temperament
- Sex
- Age
- Purebred or mixed breed
- Whether to buy or adopt

# Are You Right for a Dog?

There are important things to consider about yourself as well. Will you be a good dog owner? Here are some questions you need to answer before getting a dog:

- Do my family and I have enough money to pay for a dog's food, toys, and health care?
- Am I patient enough for a puppy who may make a mess in my room, tear my homework, eat my new sneakers, and wake me when I'm sleepy?
- Do I really have time to help walk, feed, groom, train, and play with a dog?
- Am I willing to take care of a dog day after day for many years?

If you answered *no* or *maybe* to any of these questions, DO NOT GET A DOG! If you answered every question with an honest *yes*, here are places to get more information:

- Your library, bookstore, and pet supply store have books about choosing and caring for a dog, as well as books about individual breeds.
- The American Kennel Club has information on purebred dogs. They can be reached at 5580 Centerview Drive, Raleigh, NC, 27606; World Wide Web Home Page, http://www.akc.org/akc/; E-mail, info@akc.org.
- Your local animal shelter can tell you about adopting.

# Index of Breeds

## About the Author and Artist

Stephanie Calmenson is the author of many popular books for children, including *Dinner at the Panda Palace* and *The Principal's New Clothes*. She is also coauthor, with Joanna Cole, of the Gator Girls series as well as numerous anthologies, including *Ready . . . Set . . . Read!*

Justin Sutcliffe is an award-winning photojournalist whose work has appeared in periodicals such as *Life, Newsweek, People, Time,* and *Vogue.* He has also worked as a foreign correspondent for British national newspapers, covering news in the Americas.

Together, Stephanie Calmenson and Justin Sutcliffe created *Rosie: A Visiting Dog's Story,* which *Smithsonian* magazine called "one of the outstanding nonfiction titles of the year."